The Archangel's Pen Presents

"And The Angels Walk Beside You"

"A Collection of Channeled Messages From Archangel Michael"

Book II
of The Collection:
"Archangel Michael Speaks"

Written & Channeled By Carolyn Ann O'Riley

Edited By Carolyn Ann O'Riley
Cover Illustration by Carolyn Ann O'Riley
Published by The Archangel's Pen
Carolyn's Photograph by Chris Millar

Edition II

Copyright © 2006 by Carolyn Ann O'Riley. All rights reserved. No part of this work may be reproduced or transmitted in any form or by any means, electronic or mechanical, including photocopying and recording, or by any information storage or retrieval system, except as may be expressly permitted by 1976 Copyright Act or in writing by the Author.

All correspondence and inquires should be directed to:
Carolyn Ann O'Riley
The Archangel's Pen
18794 Vista Del Sol
Dallas, Texas 75287-4023 USA
214-232-7199 Phone
972-931-0363 Fax
E-mail: channel333@sbcglobal.net
http://www.carolynannoriley.com

Library Of Congress Catalog Card Number: 00-192164
1st Edition: ISBN 1-891870-17-3
2nd Edition: ISBN 978-1-4116-9348-7

Dedication

This book is dedicated to The Creator and
The Creator's Messenger, Archangel Michael,
for their infinite love, faith, omnipresence
and guidance within each moment of this Human Entity's
existence.

Also to Archangel Raphael, Archangel Uriel, Archangel Gabriel,
 my Guardian Angels, Spirit Guides, and Spiritual Family
for their Love, protection, vigilance
and constant nudging.

To The Universe for providing the tools and abundance
to perform this service of love.

To My Children Sonia and Chris
and My Husband Pat and my extended Family both
through blood and through Light for their love and tolerance
 (it isn't always easy for others to accept and understand
when you talk to Angels), may they truly know how very
special they are to me. I love you, thank you for your love.

To the devoted readers of
Archangel Michael's Messages, and Books
Remember you are loved beyond measure.

Author's Acknowledgment

I have been very blessed to have had these messages of love and hope
channeled through me for your understanding and enjoyment.

My desire is to share the love that has been
channeled through me with you, so that it may speak
 directly to your heart,
for your own discernment and validation.

The Creator's Message is that we learn to love
ourselves so that we may remember how to
love others.

In our remembrance, of The Creator's love
we can remember who we truly are
and from whence we came.

We can change the world one person at a time
through love.

Love is all there is.

Table of Contents

Forward		Page 7
Chapter 1	Intention	Page 13
Chapter 2	A Special Meeting	Page 19
Chapter 3	The Starfish	Page 27
Chapter 4	Empowering One's Self	Page 31
Chapter 5	The Bubbles of Thought	Page 37
Chapter 6	What Judgments Do	Page 49
Chapter 7	The Tree House	Page 65
Chapter 8	The Creator's Highest Mt.	Page 73
Chapter 9	Through The Looking Glass	Page 85
Poem:	"Angels"	Page 97
Chapter 10	Angels	Page 99
Chapter 11	Until We Meet Again	Page 105
Chapter 12	Suggested Reading List	Page 109
About The Author		Page 113
Other Books & Tape		Page 115

FORWARD

Welcome! readers to some very special material that Archangel Michael has brought together for you.

He wanted the tools and messages to be available for those that are ready to really begin to examine who they truly are.

He desires to remind you that it is time to remove the veil of forgetfulness. It is time to walk the path with Spirit.

Don't be surprised if some of the ideas sound familiar to you, The Angelic Kingdom has been whispering them in your ears for eons, but not many were ready to listen to them then.

Perhaps now is the time that you are ready to work with them yourself. With your true intent to move forward you will find them to be the most powerful ways to help yourself shed the many layers so to speak of things that no longer serve your highest good.

It has been my pleasure to assist Archangel Michael to bring forth these tools and messages that He wants you remember and use.

You might find it interesting that Archangel Michael was involved with all aspects of this book project down to the way the chapters are laid out and the pages numbered. There is nothing here that He has not touched or that is not in the specific order that he suggested that it be in.

We are constantly hearing stories of how Archangel Michael's messages have been discovered by some of our readers. They met someone for the first time and were directed to our website http://www.carolynannoriley.com where they found just the guidance they needed that day; or they were surfing on the web and were lead to the website; or a friend forwarded a monthly message and the receiver found healing that was needed at the time. It is confirmation constantly to hear the many ways that the Angels are directing those that are ready to hear the messages to find them.

Most of you are not aware that The Angels are actually working through you when you forward a message with true love, friendship and intent. You are being an Earth Angel to those you forward the messages to when they themselves have given intent to move forward.

Your messages to us are precious and we thank you for letting us know how Archangel Michael's messages have touched your life.

It never ceases to amaze me and confirm that which I already know; you have been guided by your Angels to read this book. Your name is known in the Heavens whether you realize it or not and your Guidance has presented this book to you because there is something here that is to trigger what is needed for your next step. This is no coincidence or accident that this book was picked up or received as a gift by you.

This is your journey make note of where you are now on your path because upon completion of this book you will no longer be at the same fork in the road wondering which way to go. The tools and messages are here to offer you guidance. They are powerful beyond words when used with the deepest sincere spiritual intent.

Enjoy your reading and work with the tools that Archangel Michael has shared with you, allow them to assist you on your journey. In turn share them with another and watch as you both grow and glow brighter and brighter.

Never forget how much you are dearly loved, you are wondrous Beings of Light as Archangel Michael constantly reminds you.

In deepest gratitude, devotion, service and love I share these channeled gifts with you and dedicate this book to The Creator and The Creator's Messenger, Archangel Michael.

May the Peace and Grace of The Creator be with all of you as you share in the glorious love that enfolds each page.

I AM NOEOL, as named by Archangel Michael, or within this Earth Plain known as Carolyn Ann ORiley, the channel.

"And The Angels Walk Beside You"

Book II of the Collection " Archangel Michael Speaks"

Written and Channeled
by Carolyn Ann O'Riley

INTENTION
INTENTION
INTENTION
INTENTION
INTENTION

Chapter 1
<u>Intention</u>

Welcome My Beautiful Beings of Light, you were called to read this book. Did you not realize that your name is known on the other side of the veil? Perhaps you did not realize that you had set yourself this appointment to re-awaken who you really are. Within this book's pages you will find the triggers and messages that have been awaiting your remembrance. It is through re-membrance that you will find your answers to all your questions and your way Home. Each time you pick up the book feel the Angelic presence surround you for they have been communicating to you saying it is time Beloved to arise and walk your spiritual path.

My Beautiful Beings of Light, purpose, direction of action or words, are Earth Bound descriptive language that provides a partial interpretation of what intent means. Communication to others is so vastly important and subjective.

Intent is a multi fold process as the Heavenly Realm sees it. Intent would be like the chocolate coating around the caramel nugget in a piece of candy.

You visually see the piece of chocolate candy, but the center you cannot identify from outward appearance only. You begin interpreting things with your eyes first when you look at the piece of candy. You would analysis visually through your eyes the experience with candy or purport or deduce that this item was sweet. Your taste experience with candy would tell you that it tastes good to one that likes chocolate. To some candy might even fulfill an emotional need, or so they want themselves to believe, for something within their lives that they deem is missing.

Ask yourself can you see the center from only looking at the outer coating? Can you see the candy maker's intent by the first visual analysis? Can you say for certain from only the outside coating appearance that this candy only has one filling?

Many have been deceived by a piece of chocolate candy, they didn't like the fillings or didn't like the taste of the chocolate itself, but could you tell that by just looking at the piece of candy itself? Others have utilized deception to trick or injury another through their manipulation of a piece of candy by hiding nails, or broken glass, etc as evidenced in many Halloween horror stories.

Beloveds, intent is the first coating along with your actions or words that communicates to The Universe, The Creator and other Earthly Humans what actions or outcomes you are really trying to achieve.

Can other Earthly Humans misinterpret your intention, yes. Every Earth Bound Entity must translate through their internal databases what your intentions coupled with your actions and words means to them. Each individual will have a different version. Each has a separate experience database from which to analysis the impressions it is receiving from you. There are no two versions that are identical to each other, because no two individuals have had the same set of experiences within this lifetime or others. Can this database of interpretation go backwards into past life experiences of an individual, yes.

Can your intention be manipulated by you to injure another, yes.

Can the Universe, Angels or The Creator be deceived by your true intention coupled with your words and actions, no.

The intention from the other side of the veil, My Beautiful Beings of Light, is interpreted directly from your heart center. It is viewed directly from your source; it does not filter through language, emotion, feelings, past experiences, your beliefs, or others beliefs. The Universe, Angels and The Creator throw out your words because Earthly Language is far to limiting it is not used on the other side of the veil.

The Universe speaks in sound, light and color. The Universe also speaks directly to you through sound, light and color

Do those outside the Earth Plain judge your intention, no. It simply is and is recorded as found in your heart center. Beloveds your true intentions will come back to you at the end of your Earthly walk in that which you call your death process. This intention recall has also been described as a life review.

Some of you may have been reading of those that have death experiences and return to write or tell you of them. The Earth Plain calls them near death experiences, which makes us smile because there is nothing near about it. The loved one has in fact crossed over and made a decision with assistance from The Creator for whatever appropriate reason to return, perhaps it is not their time, or be it a life mission not finished, or for whatever the circumstance their life essence returns to their physical vessel.

You ask, do others judge the life review outside the Earth Plain? My Beloveds, only you the viewer judge it on the other side of the veil. You are asked by your Angels how do these scenes make you feel? The life review process is used as a measure by the Soul to gage the next set of learning and growth experiences that it desires to achieve.

So My Beautiful Warriors of Light others within the Earth Plain filter through their databases that which they are perceiving your actions, words, and deeds to mean to them. Their interpretation of that action by you, is what those within the Earth Plain call judgment, however in many cases it really is only an objective analysis of understanding, not something colored with hidden agenda by descriptive definition on the part of the other receiving Earth Plain Entity. Most analysis actions by others are simply labeling in your Earth Plain language the event or whatever it might be. If it causes issues within the other then a judgment might come forth to mask the hurt or pain that the other is feeling in response to your action.

As you begin to strip away the many layers that are impacting you and you become more in tuned and aligned with your highest good, it will be more difficult for others to perceive your actions, words or deeds as anything but of highest intention. Things will not be going through as many layers within you to communicate to another. They in turn if working on their own spiritual path will also be clearing their layers so that others will not have to go through as many layers to be interpreted.

The clearest direction and action creates the clearest intention, help yourself by asking prior to any action: "What is my intention?" "What do I really want to have happen here?" "How can I communicate this for the highest good?"

An Exercise to help you identify your intentions.

Note: *The most truthful answers will come to you spontaneously. Answer the questions by writing down the first impression that pops into your head. You may be surprised by what really surfaces:*

What has brought me to this fork in the road?

How has it affected me?

How has it affected my family?

Are others regularly misinterpreting what my intentions are?

What can I do to stop the wrong impression or intention from coloring my actions or deeds?

INTENTION
INTENTION
INTENTION
INTENTION
INTENTION
INTENTION
INTENTION
INTENTION

Chapter 2:
A Special Meeting

My Beautiful Beings Of Light each moment starts a new journey. Another rung on the spiral, a period of renewal. A period of reviewing and releasing the old that no longer serves your highest good.

With each emergence and release you are growing and becoming lighter and lighter. With each passing moment you are changing within the Heavens vision fields and sparkling more brilliantly within the cosmos.

Beams of golden light are permeating all levels, dimensions and aspects of each of your energies fields. We smile because most are not even aware of these Vibrational changes or waves of transformation and love that emanate from The Creator.

More and more are awakening bring forth more potential for change within this Earth Plain. We are so grateful to you my Beautiful Warriors of Light for embracing each other and helping all that resonate to your vibrations.

You are learning the lesson of the trees My Beloveds. You are learning that you must bend and flex with the changing winds in order to hold your place on the game board and move to the next rung of the spiral.

The tree accepts the gifts of The Creator by accepting the rain when it comes, or doing the best it can when there is no rain. The tree has faith that what is to be for its highest good will be provided by The Creator.

It brings forth its finery in foliage bearing its beauty and grandeur to The Creator, it's beautiful limbs outstretched upwards to the Heavens. It allows all that have need of it a spot of shade for those that desire to sit beneath it.

It doesn't question whether those making use of its shade are animal, feathered friend, human or a rock. It welcomes all without discrimination. The tree shares it energy fields with ease and grace to all that wish to enter its vibrations.

The tree shares all that it is for when it has no more life it even then shares it's love by changing into a different form of energy and transformation in all sorts of ways.

You my Beautiful Beings of Light are changing and the tears of joy and exclamations of "We knew that you could" are resounding in the Heavens. We are so appreciative of your efforts and work towards your transformation into that which you truly are. Continue your efforts Beloved and your future will become brighter and brighter by the moment. The Pristine Majesty of The Creator's Master Blueprint is over shadowing your progress and you cannot fail Beautiful Beings Of Light for you are in perfection within The Creator's Mind.

Allowing yourselves to open to the voice of your spiritual heart, receive your own guidance and accepting that which you truly are, is the goal towards which you are working.

You are learning that no two compare so to compete and hold yourself to another's projected mirror is futile. You are the only one in all of existence with the talent that is to come forth. You see you each have a very special piece of the puzzle that only you can provide.

Whether it is to hold the light in just a certain way within your own space or something that will affect millions, it matters not. It only matters that you bring forth that which is your gift to creation. Allow your very special gift to shine so brightly so that it illuminates the path for others to see and find their way back Home.

Angel Kisses and beautiful waves of pink and golden love light are showering you as you read this today. You are ever known by The Creator and loved and adored for who you truly are. Not one of you is ever forgotten. You are never alone whether you have invited us into your life or not we still honor you and your journey. Ask your Angels at this time to give you an Angel Kiss. You deserve all the love that is yours to receive.

I've someone special I wish you to meet this day. It is a part of yourself that has always been with you, but you have just forgotten. Journey with me My Glorious Beings of Light into meditation and meet this special part of yourself.

I'll journey with you with your permission. It gives me wonderful pleasure to assist you in remembering who you truly are.

Find a quiet spot perhaps a favorite chair, cushion or sofa where you will not be disturbed for a while. Pull a light blanket over yourself if you like so that your physical body will not be chilled and distract from your journey.

As always we ask that your ego self be the observer only on this journey, direct it to sit on your left shoulder. Request your Highest Guidance to merge with you at this time. Feel it's energy spreading forth through out your Beingness. It is bring you such wondrous peace and serenity as it merges with you.

Your Highest Guidance is requesting from The Creator a beautiful beam of white golden light to filter down streaming into the room from the corner nearest where your physical form is residing. The white golden light is entering your crown chakra and permeating all parts of your Beingness all levels, dimensions and aspects. You are now divinely protected and only those things that you give your permission to can even communicate with your at this time.

The golden white light is pulsing out from your Beingness in all directions filling all with the beautiful protecting light.

Visualize yourself entering your Heart Chakra now. You are walking around within the Heart Chakra and have located the door that you labeled on your last visit "The Door To Your Highest Guidance Within". You turn the handle cross the threshold and find yourself in a corridor with an escalator and an elevator.

The journey is best traveled by elevator. You push the button, by the way this elevator only has one button and it is, marked "up". The button is now illuminated. The elevator carriage arrives and the door opens. This time the elevator has a window on the other side that shows you the different levels that your are going through as it rises. Make a suggestion to yourself to look out the window and notice the different levels and ask your Angels to work with you on understanding each difference that you noticed on your way up at another time.

The door closes and the button has already been pushed for you, the number "9" is illuminated at this time. You begin your ascent up as you are looking out the window and noticing all sorts of differences that you are going to remember to discuss with your Angels when your return. The elevator slows and stops, the door opens on Level 9.

You step out on to what looks like some type of white platform. Your Angels and Guides are awaiting your arrival and usher you into a carriage of sorts. It appears to be a cloud formation that is shaped into a cup type shape, no top but has a side door that opens and closes.

It is floating waiting for you to enter with your Angels. All enter and the floating carriage swishes like a flash to the door right in front of your very own crystal palace. You have never been to your crystal palace from this direction before, but you think to yourself this is really fun. You ask and are told by your Angels that you can get to your crystal palace from all sorts of ways. That's good to know you think to yourself, you were really getting a little bored with the other direction.

From this direction the crystal palace appears to have an ocean view and you hear the waves breaking on the beach. You make a note to remember this so that perhaps on your next journey you can explore the shoreline and see what there is to see with your Guides and Angels.

You notice that the door still looks the same as when you last saw it. You look on the marble columns to either side to see if you recognize any of the other names that you have held in the past. Don't worry about it if this remembrance does not come. You know that all that is in perfection and the remembrance will come when the appropriate moment is in place.

You open the door and notice that many of the doors that were closed on your very first visit have been opened and explored. Many more corridors and doors are available to enter as each moment is right. You even notice a new wing that has been added. You notice and speak to the beautiful refracting light waves that dance around the room. You stand in the one that feels correct for you on this journey and make a note to yourself to explore the meaning of this color upon your return.

The Angels guide you to a door between two others that are standing open. The door is labeled "Your Solar Angel".

You open the door and you see a table with a flower vase on it. What is the flower and what is the color. Make a note to remember it and research it's meaning upon your return. In the center of the room is a golden chair. You are being lead to the chair and are asked to sit down.

The Angels manifest as you watch a large triangle in their hands. They motion to you to take hold of the triangle. As you grasp the triangle you notice that it is now filled with a solid color. This is your special color and is connected to your vibration and spiritual family.

The Angels explain that you will hold the triangle over your crown chakra in an inverted position and gently place the point into the special slot within your crown chakra that is made especially for this triangle.

There is a tingly feeling happening around your crown chakra as you insert the inverted triangle point. An expanded feeling and lightness are occurring. You discover that Your Soul is attached to the left side inverted point and now from the right point a lot of golden sparkling lights are happening and manifesting before you. Remember be kind to yourself and do not force this, if the time is not right it will be at some other moment for you, but for those that are ready to move on continue. You notice that this sparkling mass of twinkles really has no specific form, but all of the sparkles sort of stay together.

This feels so very familiar; tears of remembrance and joy begin running down your cheeks. Your Angels tell you that this is your very own Solar Angel. The Angles explain that you have now connected your three sources of guidance that you thought had been lost and veiled from you.

The mergence of another piece of who you really are has now occurred. Take a moment here to feel the love of this part of your entity. Thank it for its presence again within your existence. Ask if it has a message to share with you at this time. Give yourself some time here to communicate if it is appropriate.

Your communication is now complete and your Angels are gesturing for you to hand them back the triangle. You take it out of the slot at the crown chakra and return it to them for safe keeping; noticing as you do that the color leaves the triangle completely. It is your essence that adds the substance color to the triangle.

The Angels walk you back through your crystal palace and you exit the door. The surf is still breaking on the shore below, but your Angels say it is time to return. You enter the Cloud carriage again and are swished back to the platform. Your elevator door is open waiting for you.

You enter the elevator feeling really happy and singing knowing that you are finding more and more of yourself each time you journey within.

The elevator button marked "return" has already been pushed for you
And your descent begins. The window on the return has been closed off, but you notice that you are especially beaming and glowing.

You smile and understand that each time that you go within you are remembering more and more about yourself. You laugh out loud to yourself and say out loud in the elevator what a wonderful game this is,
"hide and seek was always so much fun".

The elevator stops and you exit into the corridor enter back into your heart chakra and return to your physical presence.

You begin stirring and when you are ready wiggle your fingers and your toes and open your eyes.

Remember all your notes of research that you want to begin doing and write them down so that you won't forget them.

I Am Archangel Michael, The Creator's Messenger of Love, Joy, Wisdom, Light, Peace & Grace.

Chapter 3:
The Starfish
Author: Unknown

Once upon a time there was a wise man who used to go to the ocean to do his writing. He had a habit of walking on the beach before he began his work.

One day he was walking along the shore. As he looked down the beach, he saw a human figure moving like a dancer. He smiled to himself to think of someone who would dance to the day. So he began to walk faster to catch up.

As he got closer, he saw that it was a young man and the young man wasn't dancing, but instead he was reaching down to the shore, picking up something and very gently throwing it into the ocean.

As he got closer he called out, "Good morning! What are you doing?"

The young man paused, looked up and replied, "Throwing starfish in the ocean."

"I guess I should have asked, why are you throwing starfish in the ocean?"

"The sun is up and the tide is going out. And if I don't throw them in they'll die."

"But, young man, don't you realize that there are miles and miles of beach and starfish all along it. You can't possibly make a difference!"

The young man listed politely. Then bent down, picked another starfish and threw it into the sea, past the breaking waves and said- "It made a difference for that one."

There is something very special in each and every one of us. We have all been gifted with the ability to make a difference. And if we can become aware of that gift, we gain through the strength of our visions the power to shape the
future.

We must each find our starfish. And if we throw our stars wisely and well, the world will be blessed.

Ask Yourself What Are My Star Fish and How May I Serve?

Write down the guidance you receive when you ask that question. Remember to put a time and date on it. You will be surprised when you come back and read it later that your intuition on this subject will have vastly changed. When you are on your Spiritual Path your are ever evolving upward.

Chapter 4:
Empowering One's Self

Note: Dearest Readers, this is Carolyn,
I have been asked to share this with you along with several other bits of information within this book. The road to empowerment of One's Higher Self is the journey that you are on.

Begin by Asking Archangel Michael to help you confirm that what you are learning and reading is indeed an acceptable truth for you. Don't just accept it to be, because it is for another, but expect a confirmation that it is appropriate or not appropriate for you at this time. This is your self-test of what is appropriate and One will benefit from learning to follow their own inner knowing in this way. Learning to trust your own knowing is a large step in empowering yourself.

Understand that nothing is a coincidence. It is synchronicity for you and part of the Creator's Master Blueprint within the Universe.

We created our contracts before we incarnated and chose our families etc. in the same way.

A visualization for you to contemplate: Visualize yourself walking around inside a large clear quartz crystal. Each thought that you think is sent directly out the terminator point and amplified out into the Universe. Each thought creates. That is what we are, creators. We create with our thoughts. What we fear draws near, what we resist persists. We will go into this more as we progress.

We are indeed a spiritual being having a human experience.

At the beginning of each reading session take a sheet of paper, title the page "Problems I'm Leaving At The Door".

Make yourself a Creator Box: on the sheet of paper write down the troubles of the day that have come into your awareness. Fold the paper place them in The Creator Box and know that you can pick up the issues once again after you have completed your reading session if you so wish. But for the time you are spending on your reading put them aside.

If you decide after your reading session that you do not want to re-saddle yourself with the problems leave them for The Creator, The Angels and The Universe to assist you with them. Know that this is done and don't bring them back up. Understand that they will be dealt with in what ever way is most appropriate for the situation within The Creator Master Blue Print and Time Sequence. Please don't be tempted to frame out how these are to be solved for you in so doing your have created limitations and road blocks, many times tying your Angels hands in assisting you.

On a periodic basis make a ceremony of this; empty the Creator Box into your BBQ Grill, Fireplace or large metal bowl or trashcan. Burn the contents and allow the Angels to take the smoke and issues with them as the flame consumes each page and issue. If you are not somewhere where these can be burned then bury them in the dirt, or put them though a shredder and know that they are being handled. Do not read them again once you have written them down and folded the paper. Say a prayer of thanksgiving and thank The Angels, Universe and Creator for their help in resolving these for you.

After writing your list of problems that you are leaving at the door, mentally and in writing and vocally if you desire answer the following question

<u>What is my intention for this reading session?</u>

Let's get those intentions out there. It's the appropriate moment to walk your talk. Your actions are to be consistent with what you say you want or you confuse those Heavenly Beings trying to assist you as well as the actions that are brought into your awareness due to your thoughts that might be betraying yourselves if not properly worded or intended.

Perhaps an intention journal might be an excellent tool for you. Make sure and date the entries making any notes that you feel drawn to make with each entry. A guess is that each time you re-read the intention that it will remind you of how much you have grown.

Here are some daily exercises to assist you in creating your day. One re-programs themselves one moment at a time. There are many layers that must be worked through. The repetition assists in step-by-step beginning to trust in yourselves.

We call this **"Soul Talk"** or **Affirmations**, repeat each statement three times:

> I Am One Unified Entity, my subconscious mind, conscious mind and super conscious mind are in perfection and aligned, balanced and in complete harmony under the direction of My Divine I Am Presence.

> I Am Centered and Walk with my Angels and Guides in pure Creator Consciousness (some call this Christ Consciousness) and directed by Divine Will

I Am Choosing Unconditional Love over fear

I Am Choosing Self-Trust over Self Judgment

I Am Choosing Abundance over lack.

I Am Choosing Now over Present, Past or Future

I Am Choosing freedom over limitation

I Am Choosing Soul Self over ego self.

I Am Choosing expansion and growth over stagnation

I Am Choosing to follow my own inner Wisdom over someone else's belief system

I Am Choosing compassion over apathy and helplessness

I Am Choosing Divine Oneness over feelings of isolation and separateness

I Am following my own inner guidance

I Am answering my own inner questions, as I know I am the only one with the perfect answers that are within my path.

I Am empowering my self with each action.

I Am Creating My Own Heaven On Earth

I Am a projection of my own Divine I Am Presence

I Am radiating light, love and harmony from my Golden Heart Center.

I Am releasing and transmuting daily my past, present and future into the Violet Transmuting Flame.

I Am remembering and utilizing the wonderful gift of forgiveness

I Am surrounded by a golden dome of protective white light and nothing but those things that I give my permission to can penetrate that energy field.

I Am expressing my thanksgiving to The Creator and expressing my constant love.

I Am finding beauty in all that I see

I Am thankful for the daily miracles that are all around me

I Am walking with my Angels and Guides

I Am that I Am, And So It IS " AUM"

Perhaps you have been drawn to create some of your own Affirmations write them here.

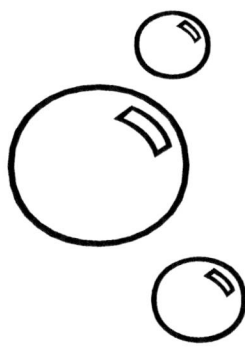

Chapter 5:
The Bubbles of Thought

Beautiful Beings of Light, much is going on about your May 5th alignment is it not. Lot's of pre-dictions and possibilities are floating within the ethers for each of you. For those that will potentially connect with the energies these can be utilized to assist you on your spiritual paths.

Alignments are potential growth steps that come highly energized and gifted with Divine Grace for your step onto the next rung on the spiral of evolution. This is there purpose. It is the Divine Essence giving those that would accept the gift, if appropriate for that participant at that appointed moment in Now, a boost up to the next rung of the spiral. The effects are those that you yourself define and label. The Higher Realm has no need to place labels or pre-dictions on these events. They are part of The Creator's Master Blueprint and are in Perfection.

As in any area some will utilize the energies to their fullest extent, some will ignore the implications that there are additional energies coming forth, some are still totally asleep thus will sense no-thing and will not understand what all the clamor is about.

Begin asking your higher guidance the question; is this alignment something that I am to participate in? Continue to query your Higher Self, if your guidance has stated you are to participate, ask for information about what effect or potential purpose this will have for you.

When pondering any question or activity, I ask each of you to begin asking your inner guidance the questions. Ask your inner self, what does this mean to you, for as we have explained before each Being is so very specialized, what would be potentially available and explained for one is not what is appropriate for all.

There are many different parts to play in The Creator's Grand Masterpiece, each participate volunteered, came forward, was selected and was assigned a part prior to your incarnation.

When others have shared a specific event with you, that perhaps could involve the many of the Whole, find a place of peace and go to your own inner guidance source. Ask how am I connected or involved with this event? Listen for your own most accurate answer for that is the only truth for yourself.

Going within on a consistent basis will keep you in tuned with your highest guidance. Then you can assimilate and discern is this event for me or is this my ego requiring that I become involved for the sake of the drama that it provides.

Remember My Beautiful Light Warriors that the ego likes the drama and chaos that it manipulates you into. Only by knowing what your Highest Guidance sounds like can you discern, is this meant for me? Or am I just to be an observer for this activity or event that is being communicated. The inner answer will also keep you from experiencing perhaps effects that you were not to be a part of the cause of by participating in something that was not for your specific highest good.

Beloveds your guidance is within not without. You are Powerful Spiritual Beings playing Human Parts in duality, governed by the rules of Earthly Cause and Effect.

As the energies become more concentrated and intense it's like turning the gas on a stove higher and higher. It produces pressure and stress so that those issues that have been hidden can come forth to be released. Ask yourself what happens when and issue comes up and is not released. Dis-ease my Beautiful Beings Of Light is one possible result. The effects could be called by so many names but it all comes back to the same issue, pain, fear and negativity must be released or it builds and intensifies.

We hate to see you in such pain my Beloveds. We at times weep for you. This Earthly experience is what you chose to do when you incarnated and veiled yourself away from your Highest Knowingness. Begin slowly to dissolve the veil, use the exercise of forgiving and releasing all that no longer serves your highest good and feel the blessed relief.

These unresolved issues are what dull your most brilliant glowing lights.

We know that you are working My Beloved Warriors of Light because the beacons of your brilliance reach us more glorious than the moment before.

Make yourself understand that you have only one moment at a time. This is what is meant by the NOW. It is the present moment in which you are participating. Use your energies to stay within that moment so that you might enjoy this beautiful gift from The Creator.

The past my Beloveds has already been experienced why re-visit it. You learned those lessons why repeat them. The future my Lovely Warriors is not yet ready for you or you would be already within that chosen potential moment. Use the gift of this moment, the

Now and allow it to be all that it is meant to be. Bring in the beauty that is all around you and feel the love and warmth that is there for each of The Creator's Children. Remember that The Creator only creates Perfection and thus keeping the self mulling through the past or fast forwarding into the future brings anxiety, not peace.

Feel our presence and know without a second thought that we are with each of you each moment, for The Creator did not place you here alone. We are your spiritual support system and we walk with you each step of the way.

We watch over you with such love that we truly have no Earthly words that can express the true intensity of what that means on this plane of existence. But you know what that love is My Beloveds because that is what you are constantly searching for.

You remember that love and it's intensity, you've just not connected it to The Creator and the you that you truly are. When you remember that feeling and it's Source you will cease looking for it in all the wrong places and relationships, for you will know in that instant that it is something that has never been missing, just forgotten until that precise awareness comes flooding back.

It will be like a light dawning within your awareness. Your higher self at that time will begin guiding your back so that you will recognize each incident when you searched and selected that which did not fill that intense need of The Creator's Love.

Ask the Angels to begin helping you by putting faces and actions with the true feeling and the Source of this love will assist you in releasing that which no longer serves you. You will go Ah Ha! that is why I selected that mate. You will understand then that you were searching for The Creator's Love, and then you will say to yourself I understand now why it did not satisfy that need. The relationship was never capable of that type of love within this Earth Plane. Your guidance or Angels will assist you in saying I no longer need this within my data bank. Say to yourself I recognize what this was all about; it no longer serves me to continue carrying this around with me I will release it and forgive myself.

With each release you become lighter and lighter. Your Angels or guidance can then assist you in addressing the next issue. This is a never ending process My Beautiful Beings of Light. You are ever growing and changing therefore releasing will be something that is needed at each step within your evolution. That is why I keep bringing you back to this point.

Bringing you The Creator's Messages of Love, hope and assisting you in your inner journey are only a few of my activities during this mission, but it is a major focus that feels me with such joy to help you when you call on me.

With your permission, this Messenger will journey with you on another mediation.

Find a quiet space where you will not be disturbed for a while. Either sit, lie down or what ever is the most comfortable way for you to participate. If you chill easily place a light cover over the physical body. We don't want the distraction of your being to cool to concentrate.

As always ask your Ego to step aside and state that it's only involvement will be to perch on your left shoulder and be an observer. Request that your Higher Self fully integrate at this moment.

Invite the Angels and Guides that are appropriate for you to be with and ask them to support you on this adventure. Feel their energies surrounding you with The Creator's Love. Feel my presence all around you and know that it is so.

From the corner of the room The Creator is sending you down a beautiful beam of white protective light, also on this journey a glorious brilliant ray of golden light laced with pink. The rays are entering your Beingness through the soles of your feet, rising up through the legs, the knees, the thighs, the abdominal area, the solar plexus, the heart and chest area, filling the arms, fingers and neck, rising into the face and head and exiting through the crown chakra. The beams are circulating through you and then back to The Creator and back through you again.

You are now divinely protected and only those things that you invite can disturb you now.

You are at peace and begin by going into your heart chakra; there you find the golden door labeled "To Your Highest Guidance". You open the door cross over the threshold into a white marble corridor. Feel the walls they are warm not cold as you would expect marble to be. Put your hand on the wall again and feel something else you have not felt before, the walls are energized and you can feel the vibrations. Your Angels are communicating to you that the more work you do the more energized these wall will become.

There is an elevator and an escalator in this corridor. The Angels are guiding you to take the escalator; you are to exit at the 7th level. They are telling you that they are further conveying you higher than the 7th floor, but you will be taking another form of transportation to the designated level.

You step onto the escalator and feel the rise in your Vibrational level as you go up each level. You turn and look at where you have been and find it holds no interest. You look towards the future and see that it holds no interest. The Now, this moment is so much more intense and interesting, you realize at that moment that if you had your mind in the past or future that you would be missing the beauty, joy and blissful feelings that you are embracing at this moment in Now.

You understand also in that instance why it is most important to take in all that is in the Now, so that an important turn will not be missed or smile that must be smiled communicated, because there will never be another moment in which to capture it. Each moment holds what is to be within that moment if not embraced it is lost forever.

You step off the escalator on to a pink cloud. You and your Angels sit on the cloud and the cloud whisks you higher and higher and higher. You feel why the Angels have selected this transportation mode because it more slowly conveys you. You are able to drink in each breath taking in the beautiful scenery. It clears your mind and brings you serenity.

The cloud stops at the 12th level. The Creator's Place of Being. You see beautiful golden gates open wide to greet your arrival. You see Angels on each side of the gate with large golden trumpets heralding your arrival. You see the tiny cherubs lining the way down the path to a lovely garden.

There is a golden glow that is emanating from the garden. You float; remember at this level your physical body and movement are non-present. You are in your true glowing light form. You look very much like a candle flame. You pass a clear pool and stop. You see your glorious reflection and feel such love and relief because you now remember who you truly are and from whence you came. You stand in front of the crystal pool remembering your true essence.

A tear falls and you feel such emotion well up. Allow it to be my Beloved, Allow it to be and know that it is so. Allow those tears of joy to run freely as you continue to gaze at your reflection. (Remember if you see no-thing at this time that this memory is not yours to have at this time, be gentle with yourself and know that it will surface when the appropriate moment is right for you.)

For those that are ready look into the pool again, perhaps you see a faint color associated with your image. This is the color of your spiritual family. This is part of your heritage. Make a mental note to remember to research that color upon your return.

The Angels guide you further down the path; you are being directed to the glow in the garden. You are enjoying the immaculate beauty that is all around you. It dawns on you again that if your mind was in the past or the future that you would be missing this most glorious moment in Now. The Angels are really bring this message back over and over to you again on this journey. They know that it is an important element in your progress and growth.

You see The Creator in all the glowing excellent that is The Creator's to capture. The Creator is positioned on the ground and thus your follow suit and do the same by sitting down on the grass. You feel how cool the grass is. You decide to face in the same direction as The Creator so that you can see what The Creator is looking intensely at.

You are looking out over a pristine crystal clear lake. It's like a reflection of a mirror looking back at you. You see the foliage and so forth all around. The thing that has you intrigued the most however are the bubble type images that are floating up from The Creator's upper most height. The Creator communicates that each thought produces the bubble like image and that each has a life, therefore it is critically important to produce only the purest of thoughts.

The Creator is looking into the lake watching each bubble as it floats after its creation. Each is crystal clear and filled with love. You can see the loving energy essence exuding from the bubble.

The Creator motions for you to try and watch your reflection as you produce the bubbles as you do with each of your own thoughts. (These are visible to the inner vision at this level of existence) You try one and notice that your thoughts are muddy colored. The Creator has the Angels collecting your muddy bubble thoughts and transmuting the energy so that it will not touch another thing. The Creator begins working with you through thought forms: love vibrations, symbols, tones, light and colors and you then see your thought forms becoming clearer and clearer. You are really excited at this point and understand that you are truly creating with your mind that which you experience.

That feeling of awareness dawning is so powerful. You produce a bubble that is filled with the most glorious crystal clear pink light. You laugh out loud and are really getting the hang of this now.

The Creator laughs with you for to see His/Her child learning by example gives such joy and pleasure. There is a warmth there and a feeling of love there that you understand does not exist on the Earth Plane. The Angels carry this beauty love energy, as do you within, if you choose to nurture it.

The Creator motions that it is time for you to return, a feeling of deep gratitude is communicated and a promise to practice what has been re-member in this visit. You additionally promise to teach and help others re-member this key piece to the puzzle.

The Angels guide you back down the path and back on to the cloud. You begin your descent very slowly so that you can feel the density and it's effects on your form as well as your mental capacity dulling. You reach the escalator once more. You have to remember to make your footstep on the escalator, and then ride back down into the heart chakra. You do not like the heaviness that you are experiencing but the Angels remind you that you promised to return and help others to re-member.

You cross back over the threshold back into your heart chakra, back into your physical form. When you are ready wiggle your fingers and toes and open your eyes. Remember to reorient yourself before going about your day. You have had some really powerful energy and you need to ground a little.

My Beautiful Beings of Light I have enjoyed traveling with you this day. Know that I am but a request away. Know too that I love you more than the words of this Earth can ever express.

I Am Archangel Michael, The Creator's Messenger of Love, Joy, Wisdom, Light, Peace & Grace.

How did this meditation make you feel? Write your impressions down here and date them.

Chapter 6
<u>What Judgments Do And Why It Takes Release</u>

Dear Ones when judgments are made one to another you bind yourselves to one another with cords and chains so to speak. The cords have barbed like hooks on the ends very much like fish hooks and secure themselves to you through the chakra system in whatever chakra the judgment pertained to.

As you are aware judgments can happen with your knowledge or without your knowledge. When you make a judgment about another you send out a cord attached to yourself with a hook and anchor it on your physical entity end, the other hooked end attaches to the chakra area of the other person that the judgment was about. Likewise when someone else makes a judgment about you, they in turn send a cord with a hook attached to themselves and the other hook that attaches itself to you in whatever chakra is applicable.

The cords remain with you until such time as they are released in any number of ways. They also have the potential to drain your energy thus damaging your health.

Releasing work is so very important to your health through out all of your dimensions, aspects and levels.

Carolyn, my messenger has been asked to share with you a number of ways in which you can assist yourselves in releasing old belief systems, the cords and chains that bind you, as well as assisting your balance and stabilization through toning, Mudras, and decrees.

Decrees My Beautiful Beings of Light announce your intentions to yourself, the you that you really are, and to the Universe.

Here are several examples of Decrees to work with. The most effective way to utilize decrees are to prepare yourself as you would for meditation find a quiet place that you will not be disturbed for 10 to 15 minutes. Focus your energies on becoming as balanced and centered as possible. Once you have yourself in the appropriate frame of mind, begin by reading the decrees on by one. Reading them out loud is wonderful if that is possible. Really place your sincere intention into them. Place major emphasis on the words " I Am" and the words "Now". Repeat the reading process three times during each session.

I decree I AM releasing all that no longer serves my highest good, NOW!

I decree I AM open, receiving, accepting and allowing my highest good, NOW!

I decree that I AM infinite love, light, power, peace, truth, and wisdom, NOW.

I decree that I AM filled with joy, bliss, ecstasy, bounty, abundance, prosperity, beauty, gifts, awareness, clarity, understanding, harmony, and balance, NOW

I decree that I AM blessed with special talents, special keys, special codes, special light packets, illumination, and enlightenment, NOW that are being activated as designated within The Creator's Divine Plan.

I decree that I AM exercising integrity, discernment, and requesting information that will direct my path NOW.

I decree that I AM discovering my inner serenity, and that I AM allowing the Universe to pour forth from an infinite number of sources grace, that is encompassing and permeating my Beingness with these infinite blessings for my highest good, NOW.

I AM giving thanks for the Angelic Messengers that grace my life with their presence and the outpouring of the infinite possibilities, infinite abundance, infinite prosperity, infinite success and all that is manifesting in my life for my highest good and the good of all concerned NOW.

I decree that I AM deserving of all good things and SO IT IS, "OM".

Releasing can take on may forms, all are appropriate so the specifics we have shared with you here please try. Find those that you sense work best for you. Perhaps you have already discovered on your own, several that work for you as well. It is good to have variations because releasing is an on going process. One will always be releasing that which no longer serves their highest good.

You are a work in progress Dear Ones you are always changing and growing.

Those that have tried the below suggestions have found them to be quite powerful.

Releasing: Exercise 1
When you are ready to start find a quit place where you will not be disturbed for a while. Focus your energies on this exercise and when you feel you are ready begin to write on a sheet of paper in great detail all that you sense you need to work with to clear, be it relationships, judgments, concerns, lacks there of, fears, hurts or perceived slights.

We would have you write and write until you sense it is time to stop. Notice
When you do stop how drained you feel. There may even be times that you would benefit by shedding tears when placing these items down in writing. Please do allow yourself to cry if you sense it is part of this process. Listen to
Your body and allow it to speak to you about its releasing needs as well.

When you have sensed it is time to stop, fold your paper. Place your hands on top of the folded paper and say a pray: "My Creator, I ask for your assistance with these issues and areas that I have written down here for You. I ask that You send your Angelic Helpers to assist me with these concerns so that they may be cleared from my Beingness, within all of my levels dimensions and aspects, past, present and now through out all directions of Eternity and Infinite. I give these concerns to you My Creator and know that they will be handled in whatever way is for my highest good. I thank you and your Angelic Messengers for your assistance, direction and counsel. I love you so much and I thank you for your Love. Amen"

We would have you either burn or bury the paper, which ever way is something that you can safely do. If burning use the fireplace, or BBQ grill, or perhaps a very tall metal trash can. If burying in the soil, dig down appropriately 3 to 6 inches. The hole need not be large just permanent.

As you are performing the burning or burying invite The Creator's Guardian Angels assigned to you to assist you. In your imagination see them placing their hands on your hands and helping you with this process. See them there with you, feel their hugs of gratitude for you see this is something that they have wanted you to do for such a very long time. Your Guardian Angels have been with you since your creation and have longed to help you. They watch as you struggle, grieve and hurt. They know that they must be invited into your life in order to assist you. They have been awaiting this invitation for such a very long time.

As you finish with the burning or burying sense how you feel. Take a quick emotional inventory and see if you don't feel like a tremendous weight has been lifted from your shoulders.

Know that The Creator, the Angels and The Universe are working on releasing your concerns and solutions to what you have turned over to them.

Know that they will be handled in the appropriate way within The Creator's appropriate time table, in a manner that will be for your highest good.

Know too that the only way that these can come back into your frame of thought is if you have given them permission to do so. So a reminder once you have turned them over to The Creator, allow them to stay within The Creator's care. Do not hold expectations of how they will be resolved, but know that they will be taken care of in what ever way is more appropriate for your highest good.

Releasing: Exercise 2
After centering, balancing and focusing your energies close your eyes. Ask the Angels in to assist you. Picture in your imagination a very, very, very deep water well. Make the image the old fashion kind of well with a bucket connected to a rope and a crank handle

and winch you have to turn to retrieve the bucket back up from the water well once it has been filled.

See your well however, as not being filled with water but with your concerns, fears, hurts, grief, worries, judgments, old outdated relationships, old belief programming that is no longer for your highest good, etc...................

Your well is over flowing with stuff that needs to be transmuted back into pure energy and realigned for your highest good.

Picture yourself standing in front of the well, take the bucket where it has been resting on the side of the well and toss it into the well. You may have to crank some on the handle for the wench to allow enough rope to be unwound to allow the bucket to reach the top of the concerns piled high within this well.

Ask that only one concern at a time place itself within the bucket. When you sense that the concern has entered the bucket turn the winch handle and bring the bucket with the concern to the surface and place the bucket back on the side of the well. Create a symbol, face, or cartoon figure for this concern if you desire to symbolize the concern.

Look into the bucket and see the symbol, face, or cartoon figure that is symbolizing this concern that has placed itself into the bucket to be reviewed and released by you. Take the concern from the bucket and place it into the palm of your hand. Look the concern squarely in the face. Dwell on this concern for a moment, allow it briefly to bring back the area that it is involved with. Reminder here, you are in control of this exercise and event do not give this concern energy over you. It is here for review, release and dis-empowerment in your life. After your have contemplated the concern, state " I thank you for the lessons that you have taught me in this life, I know longer need you in my life, I release you into The Universe to be transmuted back into pure sacred energy."

See this concern being taken by The Angels and watch as the Angels transmute this concern back into pure divine energy before your very eyes. Allow that image to be whatever is appropriate for you.

Work through this exercise as often or as needed until you reach the bottom of the well and there are no more concerns left in it.

You will be surprised to learn that there is a lotus blossom at the very bottom of the well that has been covered by this stuff for such a long time. One day you will be working away and realize that you are finally able to enjoy its beauty because you have worked through all the issues that day that have kept it from your enjoyment before.

Toning and Mudras for clearing:
All of the Universe resonates through the rippling power of rhythmic tone or vibration. Light, Sound and Color are the communication tools of Creation .

The Creator desired it to be so and breathed out the Sacred Breath of Creation, it sent forth rhythmic waves of Light, Sound, and Color that has reverberated through out all of creation from the very beginning.

"Toning" is sound and there is no specific note or key that this must be. As you make these sounds they will resonate throughout your own Etheric Chakra System, balancing harmonizing, and strengthening them as you absorb more and more Divine Light Substance.

When you begin the exercise of toning you will find your most appropriate range to utilize. One does not have to be a singer or have wonderful pitch to tone. It is a pure individualized expression of your own internal sound system. It might be wise during toning to find somewhere that will not disturb others. This is your vocal expression and it creates its own very special vibrations that are your sound make up.

"Mudras" are hand and arm expressions that are utilized to express or confirm your feelings and intent.

Re-member: (Toning/Sound) Vocalization and (Imagination) Visualization results in (Creation) Manifestation. Creation is Intent through Focused Emotion and Directed Thought.

1ST CHAKRA:
Called the root chakra, located at the base of the spine.
♦ Tribe
Stored here are the feelings about success, abundance, health, stability, security, courage,
Your body and connection to the Earth, also tribal (family & extended family) programming,
♦ Lessons related to the material world.
Old 3D Color: Red
New Color: Violet
Toning Sound: Uh (Huh)
*Mudra: Cup hands holding them close to your body (this would be the genital area)

Action: Visualize all the stored energy that creates limitation, scarcity, love/hate of the physical body, and survival issues flow out into your hands as you take a deep breath and make the vowel sound "Uh" (Huh). Take a deep breath to anchor this energy in the 1st chakra as you envision the color Violet. Sense the spiritual energy that lays coiled there and feel it as it begins to move up your Spine.

2nd CHAKRA:
Located in the naval area.

♦ **Power**

This chakra has to do with desire, sexual/passionate love, emotions, giving and receiving, our
Instinctual nature.

♦ Lessons related to sexuality, work, and physical desire.

Old 3D Color: Orange
New Color: Pink/Orange
Toning Sound: OOO (You)
*****Mudra:** Cup hands holding them close to your body in the naval area

Action: See all the stored energies of the ego desire body, which is never, satisfied; jealousy,
Envy, desire to possess, over-indulgence, addictions, flow out into your hands as you take
A deep breathe and make the vowel sound OOO (You)- focus on the sensation. Take another
Deep breath and see this chakra being flooded with the pink/orange color. The goals is to
Align with the desires of your spiritual desire body, which is always in balance and harmony with the physical, mental emotional, and spiritual aspects of being.

3RD CHAKRA:
Area: Solar Plexus - above the navel

♦ **Self**

♦ Lessons related to the ego, personality, and self-esteem.
Your emotional personal power center,
Sense of authority, mastery of desire, self-control, radiance, projections of love over fear, intentions to heal

Old 3D Color: Yellow
New Color: Gold
Toning Sound: Oh (Go)

*Mudra: Cup hands holding them close to your body right above the naval area

Action: With your intention to heal and clear this area envision all the trauma stored there flowing out into your hands, all the psychic energy you have absorbed from others down through
The ages, as well as hate, anger and fear. Take a deep breath and make the vowel sound Oh (Go)
As you release all the pain and emotional suffering you have experienced. Visualize flooding this
Area with Gold as you take back your will, authority, self control, once again able to project love
And light out into the world.

4ᵀᴴ CHAKRA:

Heart Area
♦ Love
♦ Lessons related to love, forgiveness, and compassion
The seat of the Soul
Old 3D Color: Green
New Color: Pale Pink/Violet
Toning Sound: Ah (Father)
*Mudra: Cup hands holding them close to your body in the heart/thymus area

Action: Move hands to position the seat of the Soul - anchor's the life force from the Higher Self and I AM presence in the body. Sense a release of all the pain, anguish and tightness as you forgive yourself and let go of all guilt, feelings of unworthiness, self-hatred, past present or future, in this or any other reality. Take a deep breath and make the vowel sound "ah" (Father) as you let go of all the impacted energies that have accumulated there and see them flowing out into your hands. Take another deep breath infusing your heart with the colors of pale pink/violet. Feel your heart center expand with love for yourself, all humanity and all creation.

5th CHAKRA:
Throat Area
♦ Will

♦ Lessons related to will and self expression
This is a point of power, truth and the spoken word
True communications, expression and creativity.
Old 3D Color: Light Blue
New Color: Deep Violet Blue
Toning Sound: Eye (I)
*Mudra: Turn Cup hands with fingers facing outward

Action: With hands turned cupped and fingers facing outward see all the restrictions, impacted energies which have kept you form speaking your truth, all energies of ignorance, words of judgment and criticism flow out into your hands as you take a deep breath and make the vowel sound "Eye" (I). Take another deep breath as you feel your throat being bathed in a beautiful voilet/blue color as you once again take back your power, henceforth speaking your spiritual truth, with discernment, discretion and compassion.

6th CHAKRA:
Brow Third Eye Area, Pituitary Gland
♦ Mind; Clarity

♦ Lessons related to mind, intuition, insight and wisdom,
Old 3D Color: Indigo
New Color: Iridescent Golden White
Toning Sound: Aye (Say)
*Mudra: Turn Cup hands with fingers facing outward

Action: Place cupped hands with fingers facing outward in the third eye area visualize the lower brain and activates intuition, insight, clairvoyance, perception beyond duality, wisdom and peace of mind. See all the fear, inability to concentrate, tension, bad dreams and pressure in the head flow out into your hands as you take a deep breath and make the vowel sound "Aye" (Say). Take another deep breath as you see blazing within your mind's eye a brilliant golden white color - as you attune to your inner seeing, tape into your higher wisdom and intuition.

7th CHAKRA:
Crown Area, On top of the Head
♦ Sense of Oneness of All Creation; Transcendence; Higher Love
♦ [1]Lessons related to spirituality
Old 3D Color: Violet
New Color: Light Violet White
Toning Sound: EEE (Me)
*Mudra: Turn Cup hands with fingers pointing backwards

Action: Visualize the Pineal Gland and upper brain, our connection to our I AM presence and the infinite, Spiritual Will, inspiration, Divine Wisdom. See the impacted energies of confusion, depression a sense of alienation, hesitation and lack of inspiration, or disconnectedness to your higher self and the Creator flow out into your hands as you take a deep breath and see a violet/white color permeate your brain cells as you claim your spiritual will and understanding, inspiration, unity, perception beyond space and time and a desire to be of service to humanity. A sense of oneness with the infinite.

8th CHAKRA:
Approximately 6 inches above your crown chakra
The Ascension Chakra, The rainbow bridge to your I AM presence.
Color: Iridescent White
Toning Sound: OM
*Mudra: Roll Hands at the wrists & cup the hand with fingers pointing upwards

Action: Hold in your hands all the negative energies that you have accumulated from your lower chakras and see them moving up the column of light to your I AM presence. Take a deep breath and make the sound "OM" see all the miss-qualified energy being transmuted into pure Divine Light Substance, a pure iridescent white. Forgive yourself and let ago of all negative energy you have manifested, past present or future, in this reality or in any other reality. If you are willing forgive every person who has ever projected any negative energy toward you, past, present or future. See all the parts of your Divine Self merging with your in your Heart/Soul Center. See all your woundes healed, and a bright golden light begin o radiate from your Heart Center. We now move out of and beyond the Law of Karma, The Law of Cause and Effect, into a State of Grace.

Lift hands straight over your head with wrists still touching from a "Y" and gradually move them until you feel a change, a charge or ripple of energy - you have now tapped into the Universal Oneness - The Christed Energy of The God Force. Feel this energy radiate down into your Heart Center.

Use this next page if you desire my Beloveds for a visual tool to assist with this toning exercise.

Toning Tools

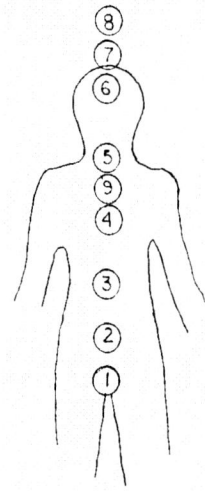

A brief added note:
A New Chakra has now come into being and would be primary labeled the Chakra of the Thymus/Heart Area with the color being: Turquoise, It works with the Soul Merge and works with the old 8th Chakra (Soul Star) and is anchored into the new 8th/9th Chakra. It's sound is not determined at this time.

Chakra Centers - Colors - 3rd Dimensional & Higher Dimensional With Toning Sound

8/9 Thymus/Heart Area Color: Turquoise
Soul Merge

8 Sound: "OM" Color: Iridescent White
Ascension Chakra - The Rainbow Bridge

7 Sound: EEE (Me) Color: Violet White
Spiritual Will, Inspiration, Divine Wisdom
Oneness with The Infinite
3D: Violet Color

6 Sound: Aye (Say) Color: Golden White
Brow - (3rd Eye) Intuition, Insight, Clairvoyance
Perception beyond duality
3D: Violet Color

5 Sound: Eye (I) Color: Deep Blue Violet
Throat communication, Self Expression, Spiritual Discernment, Power Center
3D: Light Blue Color

4   Sound: Ah (Father) Color: Pale Pink/Violet
Heart, Life Force, Divine Love from Higher Self
3D: Green Color

3   Sound: Oh (Go)   Color: Gold
Solar Plexus - Personal Power, Mastery of Desire
 Self-Control - Emotions
3D: Yellow Color

2   Sound: OOO (You)   Color: Pink/Orange
Naval or Lower Abdomen, Desire, Pleasure,
Sexual/Passionate Love,
Surrender - Tolerance
3D: Orange Color

1   Sound: Uh (Huh)   Color: Violet
Root or Base Chakra, Survival - Physical Body,
Scarcity/Abundance
Security- Grounding
3D: Red Color

How do you feel after doing the releasing exercises? Date and write your results here each time you work with these tools.

Chapter 7

<u>The Tree House Of Inner Peace</u>

My Beautiful Beings of Light, we gather this evening to celebrate another moment in Now together you and I.

Each moment is a blessing from The Creator.

Your Angels, Guides, Spiritual Family, Ascended Masters, and Heavenly Beings of Light are gathering around you whether you have cognizant recognition of their presence or not, they are hugging you.

Can you feel their love radiating out to you in all directions. Stop for a moment and concentrate on feeling that Love from them. Allow it to permeate all parts of your Beingness, all levels, dimensions and aspects. Let it filter down to the very tiniest particle of matter. It is now radiating out to all the different layers and levels that are the real you that you are.

Feel that love that they share with you. It is coming directly from The Creator through them. There is no other and there is no substitute for that loving grace, joy and bliss.

With your permission and invitation they will interact with you. They will act as a magnifier, a receiver, if you will, of The Creator's Divine Grace. It is very much like stepping up the power on a transformer. It increases the love energy that you are experiencing and they amplify the vibration to you and through you to others.

The more love that you absorb the more love that you have to share. The more love that you experience and share the more love essence that you will receive. It is a circular motion Beloveds.

The more love energy you integrate the clearer and sharper your inner vision will become.

Allow, accept and receive the inner peace. After experiencing deep inner peace you will be able to discern it from that of outer peace. Inner peace is a feeling of sanctuary. Outer peace many times comes laced with chaos of others due to the stress, fears and doubts incurred because of constant change and uncertainty of events to come.

If you are feeling pressured and off balance, find yourself a quiet space and go within. It only takes a few quiet moments. It can be anywhere; don't allow limitation to determine your ability to go within as needed. You can do it at your desk in the middle of a crowed office, know one would have to know that you are just separating your mind for a moment to go within your heart chakra. They will not even notice that you are doing anything different, only you will know, Beautiful Beings of Light. The inner peace and The Creator's Grace are awaiting you there.

Allow yourself to sense the difference that it makes in your handling the balance of that hour, then stretch that hour out into the balance of the day.

When inner peace is found the outer chaos is manageable.

If asked I can assist you further, I will wrap my blue cloak about your being and share my deep peace with you. In moments of extreme stress allow the calm to wash over you, if you but recognize it.

Learn to recognize the feelings of peace by practicing going within often. Some have become so desensitized that they no longer remember the feeling of peace let alone recognize the difference between inner and outer peace. One must remember the feeling of peace to remember the feeling of Love.

Let's practice that peace in your meditation this evening.

With your permission I will journey along with you during this meditation.

Find a quiet spot where you will not be disturbed for a little while. Sit or lie down what ever is more comfortable for you and if needed cover your physical body with a light blanket.

Ask your ego to perch on your left shoulder and only be the observer during this journey. Request that your Higher Self merge and integrate with you completely.

Begin now by relaxing the physical body, take three deep breaths and on the last breath just let the air escape in a sigh.

Begin at your feet and relax your toes, coming on up the body, your ankles, your calves, your knees, your thighs, your hips, your abdomen, your chest, your neck, your hands, arms, face and mouth. Just feel all the tension running off of your body down into Mother Earth. See Mother Earth smile and take the stress and in return she is sending your back renew cleansed energy.

From the corner of the room The Creator is sending you down a beam of healing green, transmuting gold and protective white light. It is entering through your feet and traveling up through your body exiting out the crown chakra and returning to The Creator, coming back in a circular motion through you and back to The Creator.

The energies are permeating through out all parts of the Beingness and radiating out into all parts of the room. You are now Divinely protected and only those things that you give your permission to can disturb you.

All that you invite along with your Angels and Guides are beside you on this journey. Two of your Angels will remain with your physical vessel as you travel further in your form that is the you that you really are.

Visualize as you and your group enters your heart chakra, you find the door marked " To My Highest Guidance Within" turn the handle and enter the white marble hallway.

There is an elevator and an escalator, this evening however we are going to visit a different location so you will climb the golden ladder that is to the left of the elevator door.

This ladder is going to take you to your Etheric Tree House of Inner Peace.

On each higher rung of the ladder you feel yourself becoming more calm and serene. There are 21 steps on this ladder and as you reach the 21st rung you hear a bird sing to you.

You stop and decide to listen for a moment. You see the bird, what kind is it. Remember the bird and upon your return look it up and see what message the bird was sending you.

The bird's song was so sweet. You think to yourself, "Why don't I stop and listen to the birds during the day, why am I depriving myself of this joy and this pleasure?" That bird is sending you a love message from no one other than The Creator. Make a mental note to yourself to stop and listen for a few moments each time you hear the beautiful song of the birds.

You are on the 21st rung it ends at the base floor of the Etheric Tree House platform. You think this is so much fun, I feel like I am a kid again. You watch as a glorious butterfly lands on your shoulder. It tell you " Welcome, Welcome, It has been so long since we've seen you." You see that this tree house has a door and it is marked. "My Tree House Of Inner Peace". You turn the handle on the door and enter. For those that might not be seeing the door at this time, it will appear for you when you are ready. Do not rush this process it will come when the time is appropriate.

There in the center of the Tree House room is a table. You notice that it has three chairs. Your Angels are beckoning you to sit in one of the chairs, so you do. They hand you your special inverted triangle that connects you with all your highest parts, you see your special family origin color filling the triangle as you touch the triangle. You insert the inverted tip within your crown chakra. The connection is made with all of your Beingness.

The chair opposite you on your right is now being filled with your Soul. The chair to your left is now being filled with your Solar Angel. You feel whole, completely at ease and calm now. You realize that the chaos that you felt before entering here was from separation and uncertainty. Awareness dawns and you realize also that nothing can fluster you without your giving permission to it.

In this connected environment with your entire spiritual support unit assembled, you feel infinite peace and tranquility. You understand that all you need do is quiet your mind and enter this realm for only a brief moment to regain your composure and bearings.

While you are here, ask whatever questions or for counsel or advice if you so desire. Take however long you need to do this and know that you will receive an answer in whatever way is most appropriate for you.
Within this calm your inner vision becomes much clearer and your inner hearing much sharper.

If you so desire you may ask other Heavenly Entities to visit and lend their assistance to what ever is most pressing for you at this moment. Perhaps you are feeling a bit shaky from stress overload. Ask Archangel Raphael to assist and allow his wonderful healing hand to rest upon your stressed heart for a moment, bringing it peace. If it is job worries that concern you ask Archangel Uriel to visit and turn those concerns over to him. If releasing is needed ask Archangel Zadkiel to bring his silver violet flame of transmutation and clear the area. Perhaps you might ask for my Silver Blue Flaming sword to sever a tie that is binding.

Be within this space for as long as you desire and when you are ready climb back down the ladder. Feel the heaviness settling back in at each lower rung on the ladder.

You reach the bottom of the ladder and you are back in the white marble hall. You turn the handle on the door and enter back into your heart chakra, you return to your present physical body.

Wiggle your fingers and your toes and bring yourself back into the room. When you are ready open your eyes. Give yourself a moment before going back about your day.

Beautiful Beings of Light You are Love beyond the confining words of this Earth Plane, feel the love and see its presence in all that you encounter. Look closely for the love within another's eyes; know without a doubt that it is there within somewhere, even though sometimes it is wearing a disguise.

Beloveds *I Am Archangel Michael, The Creator's Messenger of Love, Joy, Wisdom, Light, Peace & Grace.*

What thoughts and inner directions were brought to mind during this meditation? Write and date the experiences you have each time here.

Chapter 8
The Creator's Highest Mountain Peak and Crystal Lake

Peace be with you Beautiful Beings of Light as we walk together on this spiritual path.

There are more of you joining us in this walk each day. The Creator is so very proud of you for standing in faith within The Creator's waves of Light.

Visualize if you will that you have linked hands with each other one right after the other and see how you cross the globe that you thought was so vast. Dear Ones that line of Light Beings is now reaching all around the globe and is creating laps again and again encircling and enfolding Mother Earth

Mother Earth is smiling at you and is beaming back to you, her love and steadfast devotion.

We have sent you more Angels as each voices a request for more. They open their wings and reflect back to you your awesome brilliance and magnificence. This brilliance is reflecting off of the Heavens and bouncing back towards all those that have joined hands and stepped forward in their own empowerment. It is quite an awesome thing to view, all of these hugh beacons of light emanating up and joining with all the others as it reaches The Creator with your love.

The view brings spiritual tears of joy to our spiritual hearts and to know that you can accomplish this great feat in such density displays exemplary courage on your part. The density is lessening in each moment due to your deliberate intent to bring Heaven to Earth, and so it is Beloveds.

We ask that you continue with your progress, growth and remembrance. We ask that you share with those that resonate to this beautiful energy so that they may assist and add their brilliance. This in turn brings more and more to the forefront increasing the effect exponentially adding to the beautiful wave of light covering the globe

Remember to look for the beauty that is all around you. Each detail of beauty that you recognize displaces something that you felt you had lost. Each moment of sharing with others that which you have found, erases a feeling of lack. Each releasing exercise that you do heals and seal out the negative thought form that was assigned to that experience. A quick note of remembrance here my Beautiful Beings of Light when you release an experience do not allow yourself to accept it back by thinking that it is not gone. Know that it is, without a doubt.

Each fear (false evidence appearing real) that you walk through releases the hold that that fear had upon you. It has lost its power Beloveds it can no longer overcome you without your permission.

Each tear that you shed for something or someone lost can be reversed and healed with your remembrance that all are ONE and nothing can be lost it, only changes it's energy pattern and location. You are part of the WHOLE and thus will never be lost or separated from The ONE.

Even those my Beloveds that you sense will never change are within the ONE, they are a part of the WHOLE it doesn't require their permission, it is a Universal Fact, it is within The Creator's Master Blueprint. The Creator is in perfection and has lost no-thing. No-thing is separate from The Creator. The Creator is The ONE the WHOLE, the I AM that I AM.

Doesn't that make your heart smile Beautiful Beings of Light, to know that all those that you are concerned about will never be left behind. They might not necessarily be enlightened, they may not ever acknowledge the presence of The Creator, but they will never be left behind on this evolutionary spiral that is only going up. The Creator doesn't require acknowledgement to unconditionally love ALL.

The most negative Being or darkest of Soul has a spark of The Creator within, only waiting for something to ignite it's remembrance. It has to choose to be the light within itself and give itself permission to embrace the light, but it is never lost. It at some point may be transmuted back into pure energy, but that only changes it's energy structure Beloved Ones. Changing its energy structure only folds back within itself, back into the ONE.

The ONE, The Source of all, that each is a piece of, down to the tiniest particle within all levels, dimensions and aspects. This includes all the various kingdoms or species of energy, for all is pure energy, it is just changing forms and shapes.

With your permission lets participate in a meditation together.

For those that feel reservations here about this journey or are concerned because they are not visual or fall asleep when trying to mediate, know that whatever is for your highest good is all that is requested here. Only those things that are for your highest good will surface without your permission.

For those that fall asleep know that whatever level is in need of this meditation will receive the benefits it matters not if you fall asleep.

For those that are not visual, just allow and receive what is available for you here. Do not strain, whatever is to be for your benefit will be received and experienced in whatever way is most appropriate for you.

Those that are feeling apprehension about this material or meditation put it aside it is not meant for you at this time. When you are ready the material will surface again in whatever way is most appropriate for you.

We ask that all use your discernment filters and only work with those things that resonate with your Beingness.

Let us go forward.

At this time invite in your Angels, Guides, Ascended Masters, and all that you desire to join you on this journey.

Find a quiet spot where you will not be disturbed for a while. Either sit or lie down whichever is more comfortable to you. Cover your body if you chill easily with a light blanket, we want no distractions while we journey together.

Ask your Ego self to perch on your left shoulder at this time. It will only be a spectator on this venture.

From the corner of the room, The Creator is sending you down a ray of pure white light, a ray of luminescent pink, a ray of luminescent aqua blue, and a ray of golden transmutation light. The rays are entering through the soles of your feet, going up through your body filling your body fully it is exiting your crown chakra and being returned to The Creator and coming back down through your feet in a circular motion back up to The Creator.

You are now divinely protected and only those things that you have given your permission to can disturb you at this time.

Two of your Angels will stay with your physical form and keep it company while we journey.

Your pure energy essence along with your invited quests are traveling into your heart chakra at this time. You have located the golden door that says "To My Highest Guidance Within" you turn the doorknob and cross the threshold.

You find yourself in a white marble corridor you see the elevator, the escalator and the golden ladder. There is a table with a mirror on the wall. There is also a flower vase with the flower of your choice.

Look at your reflection in the mirror and remember it.
Speak to the flower and greet it with love. Ask the flower to share with you its message. Thank it for the message and we travel on.

There is a new door that you have not seen in the corridor before. It is made of pure gold and has a label that says " The Creator's Highest Mountain Peak and Crystal Lake"

You and your invited guests walk towards the door and open it. You cross the threshold and cannot believe what you are experiencing.

In front of you is the highest mountain peak you have ever seen. At this vantage point at the base you cannot see the lake. You notice that there is an arched rainbow bridge for you to cross over and there are many many steps leading to the summit of this mountain.

You walk on the golden grassy path that leads you and your party to the rainbow bridge. There is a sign at the entrance to the bridge "Leave all of your worries, problems, and concerns within this large jar before crossing". You do as instructed.

Immediately you feel such weight being lifted off of your shoulders and body. Oh! It feels so good to be free of those areas of concern. Stretch and bend and twist to allow the feeling to really settle in of being free.

Right in front of the rainbow bridge is a silver violet flame. Your Angels and Guides are motioning for you to stand within the flame. This flame will not burn you, it actually has a cool pulsating feeling. You do as instructed and stand within the flame. The flame at first has a silver violet hue that changes to pure white. When the flame changes to pure white your Angels and Guides direct you to cross the bridge.

You enter the bridge and the various colors intermingle with your energies. It is most enjoyable to feel the differences that each color can share with you. Select one that you particular like the feeling of and remember it, upon your return look up the color for the message and meaning to you.

On the other side of the bridge you begin to climb the steps. You feel lighter and lighter at each higher step. It takes you a while but you reach the peak of the mountain and feel absolutely no exertion or tiredness at all. As a matter of fact you felt like you were floating up the mountain most of the way.

Your last step and then you see it. It is breath taking at the very peak of this mountain is a Crystal Lake stretching out before you. It looks as if it has no sides and is just suspended in the air.

Your Angels and Guides motion for you to sit right at the lakes edge on this plateau, located at the summit of the mountain. You take a seat on the ground. You notice that a calming energy is entering you here as you sit. What an interesting sensation this is. Such a beautiful pulsing calming energy is coming up from the ground and working within your energy fields to bring you this glorious peace. The feelings of joy are mixed in with this peace and you recognize the feeling from a distance point in the past emanating directly from The Creator.

You find yourself uttering the words "Thank You, Thank You My Creator, and I love you so much too!"

Your Angels and Guides are instructing you to close your eyes, and say " My Creator, I AM giving my heart to you NOW, My Creator I AM giving my heart to you NOW, My Creator I AM giving my heart to you NOW " and so it is. You feel a love wash over your entire Beingness and know that your gift and intention has been received and cherished by The Creator.

The Angels and Guides now bring the large jar that you left before crossing the bridge. They have encased this jar in a large golden box so that nothing within it can dampen your experience here.

They ask your permission to take this container within the box to The Creator to allow The Creator to transmute and work with each problem and concern enclosed there.

For those that have not given permission, know that these will be taken back to be picked up upon your decent from the mountain.

For those that give permission, you see your Angels and Guides soaring into the Heavens with this contained jar within the box. They actually don't have to go very far since you are on The Creator's highest mountain peak. The Creator sends you down a note and thanks you for depositing these areas of concern with The Creator. The note says, " My Beautiful Child, I have been waiting for you to do this. I will take these issues and transmute them for you in whatever way is most appropriate for you within My Divine Plan and Master Blue Print. Know My Beautiful Child that you may do this at anytime. I do not want my Children burdened down with these concerns. You cannot feel my love for you within the density that the concerns create. I love you more than your limiting human language can express, feel My love as I share it with you here."

The tears of joy and relief are just pouring down your cheeks. Your Angels and Guides embrace you and you hear them say " There There, There There, you are so dear to us, it has pained us so long to see you suffering so needlessly with these issues. Please always allow us to assist you in clearing these from your energies fields."

The last of the tears flow down and with that last tear comes a calm that you have not experienced in a very long time. You feel that you remember this from some where very very far back in your psyche.

The Angels and Guides are bringing you a basket of Love Stones. You look at the rose colored stones with a question in your eyes. The Angels and Guides pick up a stone and show you that you add your intent by holding the stone in your hand and generating a loving thought that permeate the stone. You toss the love-imbued stone out onto the crystal smooth lake. They show you that your intent and love are then spread out to all that you encounter through each ripple that the water makes. Because the lake has no sides or limitations the ripples continue through out eternity with your love intent.

You ask to try one. This is so much fun you think to yourself. You take a stone permeate it with love and toss it out onto the crystal smooth lake. You watch as the ripples begin and continue, and continue and continue and have no visible ending.

You continue to do this and really are having a great time, and it dawns on you not only are you doing it here but your energy field interacts with all other energy fields of all that you encounter. You now understand the connections.

You understand when you clear your own Beingness of the issues and negativity that you then can enhance another's energy field with your clearness and light vibration. You know within your heart that you can assist the planet in keep yourself clear so that more and more light can filter to and through you out to others. Through your energy field that has been cleared, you can assist another by raising them up, so that they may hear their highest guidance.

Oh! The serenity and joy that this revelation brings. You turn to the Angels and Guides and tell them "thank you, thank you" you look toward the Heavens and say "thank you, thank you. I understand now, thank you for this gift".

You know it is time to return, even though it has been so fun and the energy is one that you really are having a difficult time pulling yourself way from. You know that this is something that you were allowed to experience so that you could bring this practice back and help others by your example.

Your float back down the mountainside, back across the bridge, bid the playful colors within the rainbow, goodbye until next time and exit back at the point where the jar sits. For those that allowed the clearing the jar is empty. Those that did not allow the clearing you are feeling the effects and contents of the jar rejoining your energy fields. That feeling for those that did not release, a description isn't necessary, you are understanding the effects and do not like it how they make you feel.

You walk back down the path, open the door, cross back over the threshold into the white marble corridor. You see your reflection in the mirror and see the golden light waves emanating from your Beingness. The image feels so very good and you smile. You greet the flower again and tell it until next time. You open the door cross back over into the heart chakra. You come back into your body; wiggle your fingers and your toes, allow yourself to fully settle back in before going about your activities. You have been in the very highest of ethers and it will require some grounding on your part to reorient before resuming your activities.

I love you so much and I thank you for your love. I bring you these messages of The Creator's peace.

I Am Archangel Michael, The Creator's Messenger of Love, Joy, Wisdom, Light, Peace & Grace.

What were your Angels and Guides Whispering in your ears here? Write down and date your experiences each time. Come back and read them and see how far you have grown.

Chapter 9
<u>Through The Looking Glass</u>

<u>Note</u>: *We ask that you put this message through your discernment filters just as we ask you to put all through your discernment filters. Only embrace that which resonates with you and ask for confirmation that this message is indeed appropriate for you at this moment in Now.*

Beloved Beautiful Beings of Light we come together again to journey further within your inner knowingness.

Each time you elect to take this journey your awareness expands and your frequencies rise. You gain more brilliance and splendor that reaches to The Creator in it magnificence.

What a joy and experience it is to watch The Creator become elated with such bliss to see his/her children growing brighter and brighter each moment in Now. Our gratitude overwhelms us as we hug you individually and collectively for your devotion to change what no longer serves the One and The ALL.

Each time you read these messages envision yourselves joining with all the others that are reading these messages. Your intent will make it so. This in itself will intensify the brilliance as it rises up into the ethers to grace The Creator's Presence with your love. It matters not that all are reading these messages at different times and in different places all over the globe; your intent will place it into the joint moments to accomplish this feat.

How many have been feeling the changes that were embraced by the ALL in the last celestial configuration in May? Have you seen that what was causing you grief before this event in May has increased ten fold so that you will at last have to notice it and release whatever it was that was the issue? Have you noticed as well the increase of what seems like time speeding up? Have you realized that you wishes, whether positive or negative are materializing before you at a much more rapid pace? For those that have not quite gotten to this point yet have you seen that, that which you draw towards you, in your thoughts and actions is reeling back at you almost instantaneously these days? There is very little space to breath between one crest of the wave and the next, so to speak.

The increase in the light waves coming into the Earth Plane my Dear Ones has created this effect. The more light energy that comes forth the faster the pace and more clearing that will be accomplished. The light waves are on an accelerated scale so that more and more clearing can take place.

The more negativity that is cleared the higher the frequency and the faster your evolution. We have heard your cries, your requests, and your prayers and have answered them with more light and love. The request of the few has multiplied by the thousands and now the millions all working towards the higher evolutionary spiral.

Thank you Beautiful Beings of Light for the continued clearing and cleaning of this most beautiful Earth Plane. Once again the Earth Mother is seeing hope that the Children that reside upon her are concerned about their actions and wish to correct that which was intolerable and abusive to Her and to themselves.

That crack in the veneer around the Earth Plane, if you will, has widened so that it now is completely opened for all to see; nothing can hide within the shadows any longer for the light is flooding in to illuminate The All. The All has been heard and the way selected. Those that do not desire to allow the light to illume their Beingness will indeed have a very difficult row to hoe, so to speak.

These are the moments within your soul that have been spoken of and that prophets have written about for centuries. They will happen differently though Beloveds because of all your efforts, light, love and faith to make them thus.

Your remembrance of how to clear and release that which no longer serves you is the reason for the change Dear Ones. Your inner work is paying off in Divine Grace and changes within The Creator's Master Blue Print due to your intent to make it so.

We are grateful for your courage to come face to face with that which you fear. We stand beside you and behind you as we walk together through each point that must be surmounted to take you towards your next step on the spiral.

We understand that it seems like baby steps, but the intent is increasing in volume and thus as the light intensity grows so will the magnitude of the change that will be felt in faster progression in much larger arenas. Change is happening all around you and you can join in and ride the wave or allow it to tow you under Beautiful Warriors of Light in despair. This is what you are seeing is it not?

When you are in the midst of intense pressure and stress, take a brief moment to go within your Heart Center and tell The Creator " I AM surrendering to you Now, I AM surrendering to you Now,

I AM surrendering to you Now", then take a deep breath and allow The Creator's Peace to fall around you, to walk you through one more hurdle.

This action gets yourself out of your own way Beloveds, so that Your Higher Guidance can take over the driving, assisting you through the current moment that seems out of control and unbearable.

We want you Beautiful Beings of Light to call in the Angelic Calvary, if you will. You were not placed here to have to endure the daily negativity that you have created for yourselves. This can and is changing on a moment by moment by individual by individual basis one prayer, one request at a time. It took eons of time to create this density mass, it will take every ones undivided intent and attention to clear it. This is where you are at now Beloveds, clearing all that has taken eons to create.

We are so very proud your courage and determination to do the job that you were called to do prior to your incarnation within this Earth Plane. There truly will be many stars within your Crown of Glory when this assignment is through and your graduation has been completed within this Earth Bound Classroom. We hug you and congratulate your progress once again, as we tell you one more time, Job will done. You are making a difference and you are so very dearly loved.

Let us embark once again on a journey to further your inner work.

Note: Do not be concerned Beloveds for those that desire not to journey past this point at this time. Honor your inner guidance, if this is what you are being told, for this experience perhaps is not quite ready for you yet, but for those that feel that it is, please continue.

Call in all those that you would have accompany you on this adventure. With your permission I will join you along with your most devoted servants, your Guardian Angels.

Select a quiet space where you will not be disturbed for a while. Either sit or lie down, it matters not. Our only concern is that you are comfortable in what ever position you desire for a short time. You might wish to use a light cover if your physical body chills easily for we want no distractions due to chilling of the physical vessel.

Ask your ego self to be the observer only on this journey. Direct the ego self to sit on your left shoulder and be the witness only. Request that your Higher Guidance merge with you at this time.

Mentally voice your intent for The Creator to send down from the corner of the room a beautiful protective ray of White light. Visualize that The Creator has answered your request and is also gifting you with not only a white ray but a golden ray as well.

The white and gold rays are entering your physical vessel through the soles of your feet, traveling up through your feet through your ankles, calves, knees, thighs, hip area, abdomen, chest, neck, arms, hands, fingers, face, and exiting out of your crown chakra, returning to The Creator and back down to you in a circular motion. Completely filling your physical vessel with white and golden protective light. These rays radiate out from your physical vessel completely permeating all the areas of the room you are occupying.

You are now divinely protected and only those things that you give your permission to, can even communicate with you now.

One of your Guardian Angels has elected to stay with your physical form while your other Guardian Angel motions to the you, that you really are, to take their celestial hand. Visualize yourself now being guided into your heart chakra.

You see the golden door that the Guardian Angel is pointing out that says " To My Highest Guidance Within". You turn the handle and cross the threshold into a corridor with walls of warm white marble. Note that we said warm white marble, because your inner work has energized this space and filled it with your intent to evolve.

There is a golden birdcage on the table with a lovely bird that is singing at the top of its lungs. Its singing started the moment that you elected to cross the threshold. It is welcoming you to this adventure.

Your Guardian Angel is requesting that you pick up the birdcage by the top handle, for it will be journeying with you this time.

You pick up the cage and turn around to the Guardian Angel and it is motioning for you to open the door next to the escalator on this trip.

You open the door and feel a wash of the freshest air you have ever breathed greet you as you cross over the threshold.

The door way has opened into a lush green glade. A hundred feet away over a golden bridge you see a Crystal Pyramid that you are told you will be visiting today.

The bridge has two Angels one on either side of the entrance they are requesting that you stand in the silver violet flame that is located at the bridge entrance. This flame they remind you is a clearing and cleansing flame, cool to the touch and will not harm you in anyway. They are telling you this is most sacred ground and they suggest that you be as clear as possible to enjoy this adventure to your fullest potential. They ask that any troubles, worries, or concerns be left with them in the large baskets on either side of the bridge entrance in their care until you return.

You fill the baskets and after each that you allow to be deposited within the basket you feel lighter and lighter. It is so freeing and elating to have them taken off of your shoulders even if only for a little while.

The Angels hold your birdcage as you step into the silver violet flame and see the flame change from dark violet and silver to silver and white as all is cleared and cleaned for you journey. You are motioned across the bridge as they hand you back the birdcage.

You feel as though you are gliding now. It requires no effort to move just think that you wish to move in the direction of the Crystal Pyramid and the you that is really you, floats towards it.

You have arrived at the door of this beautiful light refracting structure. You see two golden posts one on each side of the door. For those that are ready, look on each post and see how many names you have held during your past incarnations. Do not be alarmed Beloveds if you see nothing at this time. These experiences will come when the appropriate time is right for you to have these things revealed to you.

You may even see the name that was gifted to you at the moment of your birth into the Universe. You may even hear your name being whispered in your ear by the One that greeted you at the moment of your birth. Listen closely, if the time is right, hear and remember the One that named you breath the glorious sounds of your name into the ethers. Remember the celebration that took place at your birth and feel the love that created your perfection.

Feeling filled with joy and delight you open the door to the Crystal Pyramid and walk in. You see the light refracting off of all the walls and the colors dance around you welcoming your return. They say Welcome!, Welcome! Join us in this celebration of your return to these glorious halls of remembrance.

You enjoy interacting with the colors, it is so much fun to stand within one and then the other. Each has a message for you; remember to look up the color meaning of each upon your return.

The wonderful bird in the cage is still sing glorious notes with its tiny voice. Its song is ever changing.

You see off to your left many doors, most of them are open, and each has a label.
The Angels are guiding you to a door that is not yet opened and as you glide towards it you can read the name clearly it says "Through the Looking Glass".

You open the door and see a room of mirrors all shapes and sizes they cover every wall within this space. They do not however show any images as this time. How strange you think to yourself, what is the purpose if they do not reflect your image?

The Angels explain that each mirror has a special purpose and a special gift to show you where you have been and the last mirror shows you a glimpse of your potential future self. Please note here Beautiful Warriors of Light some are ready for these revelations and some are not. Do not feel offended if you see no-thing at this time. These are bold steps and not all may be ready for these remembrances. Be kind to yourself and do not strain to see. They will come when the moment in Now is appropriate for each.

Your Angel takes the birdcage and demonstrates that you must step through the mirror thusly to see what is to be revealed to you. You begin at the first mirror.

You are shown scenes from your most recent past life, scenes that have a particular impact upon your present life. You understand that each life at this point acquires skills and lessons that are to be carried forward. Some are positive lessons and images and some will make you cry perhaps. Some will show you patterns of behavior that you've selected to return and correct. It will also show you a gauge of progress that you've made.

You come away from the first mirror and feel a sadness that you do not understand. The Angel tells you to continue to the next mirror.

This experience continues until you have visited all the mirrors or until you desire not to see anymore for the moment. You can revisit at anytime, you have remembered the way now.

For those that have completed all the mirrors except the potential future you have been most brave and sense a great awareness and understanding of what you are to accomplish during this lifetime comes forth. We honor you for your courage.

The Angel motions for you to step into the potential future. This time the Angel joins you. The Angel tells you that what you are about to see can change in the blink of an eye because so many events hinge on each choice within yourself and others that effect this possibility and outcome.

Your present expanded awareness has even colored your potential future the Angel explains and you have seen this for yourself in how all has affected you though out this experience.

The Angel further explains that at the time of your initial birth of creation you were never to have the stress and despair that you find your present incarnation to be holding for you. The Angel shows you the visions that you could hold if your inner progress and awareness continues to expand.

You finish this glimpse and step back through the looking glass. You feel such awe and reverence for yourself and all others. What you just witnessed was glorious and joy filled, such bliss and rapture are yours to experience.

You understand now The Angels concerns for those within the Earth Plane. You understand The Creators tears for his/her children because you have just witnessed the perfection that The Creator had in mind for you alone. The tears of joy are flowing down you face now and you are sobbing harder and harder understanding that you have much work to do to reach that potential.

It is time to return your Angel is telling you.

You glide back down the hall and out the door of the Crystal Pyramid. The Angel hands you back the birdcage and asks you now to release the bird that has been caged within. The Angels explain to you that you have been the bird that was housed in that cage of limitation. You have now the courage to face "you" and are now free to choose to not limit yourself any further. The Angel asks you to take the empty birdcage back as a reminder to yourself that you are the only one that can limit yourself in any way.

You walk back down the path. The bird that is flying free now lands on your shoulder and nuzzles your ear. It tell you thank you, thank you for allowing it to fly free and do the mission that it was created to do.

You elect not to pick up the troubles and issues you handed over to the Angels care, but to allow the Angels to transmute them and resolve them with your permission.

You smile as you open the door back into your heart chakra. You place the birdcage with the door open next to the flower vase on the table within the White marble corridor. It will serve as reminder to yourself of the freedom that you choose when you walk within your mission here upon this Earth Plane. It will be a remembrance that only you limit your own potential.

You rejoin your physical vessel, wiggle your fingers and your toes and open your eyes. Allow yourself to ground and re-orient yourself for your have been on a very long adventure.

Beautiful Beings of Light you have viewed yourself within your past moments, your present moments of awareness and your potential future moments of awe. Allow yourself to embrace what you have witnessed and use it to further your mission and growth within this incarnation.

We love you most intently and more than any Earthly words can express.

I Am Archangel Michael, The Creator's Messenger of Love, Joy, Wisdom, Light, Peace & Grace.

Are you surprised by what you saw? List the details and date your experiences here each time you work with this meditation.

ANGELS
By Carolyn Ann O'Riley

At the edge of dawn
The Angel waits.
Hoping for an invitation
To our inner state.

Peace they bring us,
Love Divine
Beauty and Wonder
Their hearts so kind.

God is waiting
His/Her arms to enfold.
He/She whispers in our ear,
"Of My Love I have told."

We are rising to the moment
Our time is at hand.
The way is clearly marked.
United we stand.

Peace I give you,
Joy abounds,
Angels all around us,
Let our hearts feel the sounds.

Bliss and blessings, to us all.
Angels guide our way.
Heaven is above us,
They are expecting us today.

©Copyrighted Material
From: **"Go Within Feel The Love"**
By Carolyn Ann O'Riley

Chapter 10
<u>Angels</u>

Take a moment to read some information on the Angels. One must realize that it is only the "Physical Human Ego" that requires labels and levels. There really are no such limitation or classifications within the Angelic Realm to separate them only levels of responsibilities or areas of work if you will.

You might find it helpful to know that there are thousands upon thousands of Angels each having specific talents and gifts that you can call upon at all times.

As you see labels here think of them as descriptions or job types if you will and this will assist with the "Human" understanding of what these labels are that are oftentimes placed upon the Angelic Realm and along with the true meanings.

Angles have always been within Creation. One has at least two Angels that love and are with one at all times. One may request as many Angels as one would like. You can also request that they stay with you as long as you like.

You may even request Angels for others, Mom's especially should ask for additional Angels for their children.

Many Angels are playing human parts at this moment in Now.

You are Beings of Free Will, and therefore must give permission to allow anyone or anything to communicate or impact you in anyway.

The Angels thus must have your permission to interact with you.

How do you invite the Angels to come into your lives?
Ask them and intent that it be so, either through your mental communications skills of telepathy, verbally asking them, or perhaps just writing them a note. All works.

Ask for a confirmation of your invitation and expect and answer. Your answer might come as a book falling off of the shelf with a page they might wish you to read. It might be a word in a TV show that they want you to hear. Don't put expectations or place limits around the method of how you are to receive this confirmation. Allow them to communicate in whatever way is appropriate and for your highest good.

Will they give you their names? They might, ask them.

Angels come from all walks, hierarchy is not an important issue, except within the Earth Plane again due to the Human Ego. The Ego is trying to label and put into perspective how these beautiful entities fit into your self confining criteria.

This Messenger will elaborate here, to describe, if you will, the Three Hierarchies and the Nine Choirs of Angels. Here again think of the classifications as job titles or descriptions of skills and attributes, not higher or lower. importance.

| **The Throne of The Creator** |||

HIERACHIES	CHOIRS	KEY WORDS
Supreme Hierarchy	Seraphim Cherubim Thrones	Burning with Love Keepers of Wisdom Judgment/Constancy
Middle Hierarchy	Dominions Virtues Powers	Administrators of God's Will Courage/Miracles Law of Cause & Effect
Lower Hierarchy	Principalities Archangels Angels	Religions, National Leaders God's Urgent Emissaries Guardianship/Service

The name Seraphim is translated from the Hebrew meaning, "to burn" and from the Greek, "the flaming ones". The Seraphim burn with the most intense energy of divine love. To invoke the Seraphim is to request the highest most intense level of creative burning love.

The Hebrew meaning of the word Cherubim is "splendor of knowledge". The Cherubim emanate the wisdom of The Creator. They are the keepers of wisdom. They assist in intoning the spirit of truth so that every living entity is nudged with the spirit of evolution, re-growth and rebirth. If you invoke the Cherubim you are asking for the power of knowing and using the wisdom of The Creator.

The Thrones can teach you to use wise discernment in your lives. They work with the glory and equity of God's observations and are known for their dominant characteristic of steadfastness. When working with the Thrones you are asking for guidance in fairness, observation, evaluation and discernment.

The Dominions oversee the activities and duties of the angels. The administrators of the Will of the Thrones. Dominions are The Creator's "Design Department", for it is within these areas where plans for the unfolding for life begins. If confused about life's evolution ask for guidance from the Dominions.

The miracle wonder workers are the Virtues. The Virtues exemplify the essence of spiritual integrity and are known for making the impossible appear out of no-thing.

The Powers oversee the Laws Of Cause and Effect. If you're feeling overwhelmed by negativity around you and you have experienced what you perceive to be constant attacks, call on the assistance of the Powers.

The Principalities realm is over nations, provinces, and rulers. Their interests are humanitarian in nature and the fulfillment of the divine plan for individuals, nations and the planet. Their intent is not to direct or police policies, governments or individuals, but the positive nudging and guidance to select the highest decision for the good of all concerned.

The Archangels are those most familiar to humans as they are the messengers sent on missions of the utmost importance. Additionally they serve as the interpreters between the other Angelic Orders and humankind.

The Archangels overlay the Divine Seal on all things, whereby the Universe is then the Master Blue Print of The Creator. The Archangels impart and communicate to the soul the spiritual light through which it may learn to read this Divine Plan, and also to know and use for its highest good for its own faculties.

The Angels are in service to all humans and to the things of Nature, purifying and uplifting them. There are a multitude of Angels performing services for human kingdom at all times, some perform specialties that make The Creator's higher energies more accessible to you on Earth. Three that are included here are the Angles of Spiritual Fire, Solar Angels, and the Angels of Karma.

Angels of Spiritual Fire work directly with individuals who desire to use the spiritual flames. Spiritual Flames are non-physical flames, composed of the colors that correspond to the Twelve Rays that can be visualized in meditation and used to transmute negative energies.

Your Solar Angels act as a stepping down unit for the vibrations of the frequencies of The Creator's Solar Perfection so that those on Earth can receive and integrate it into yourselves. You are able to use these stepped down energy frequencies to visualize perfect health, youthfulness, magnificent beauty, and glorious abundance. All of the wondrous desires that The Creator has for you are part of this gracious service that the Solar Angels so loving perform for all.

The Powers govern the Laws of Cause and Effect. The Angels of Karma work directly with Humans to assist us in understanding the relationships of Karma within our lives. Karma is the recognition and lesson known as Cause and Effect. The Angels of Karma assist us in remembering that we volunteered for this Earthly assignment. They help us accept that we are responsible for all of our actions and that life is a classroom that we have given permission to learn within.

Ask for guidance from your Angels and ponder this question: In knowing that you are Beings of Free Will and therefore you have had to grant permission prior to anything effecting you, how then can you possibly think yourselves to be anyone's victim.

Ask the angels to come into your lives and allow their love and joy to enfold and fill you with their light, devotion and love, all just for you. Allow them to assist you in your journey of remembrance of who you really are.

Allow yourself to feel the love that belongs just to you; it has not been lost, just forgotten.

I Am Archangel Michael, The Creator's Messenger of Love, Joy, Wisdom, Light, Peace & Grace.

Chapter 11
Until We Meet Again

My Beautiful Beings of Light your way may be rocky and your spiritual eyes may not always see what is really there, but the Heavenly Realm wants you to understand and know that you have your most perfect answers within.

It has been one of the Angelic Realm's major goals to assist you with your practice and remembrance of how to go within yourselves to find the resources that have always been there for you.

The Angelic Realm come to assist you in feeling the essence of The Creator's Love once more so that you will find the strength to break free of the veil that covers your spiritual eyes of remembrance.

The Angelic Realm is here nudging to help you find the courage to restrain and retrain your Ego Self to only be the observer so that your Highest Essence can merge with your Beingness. This will once again assist you in the connection to your total true Self.

The Angelic Realm is your greatest supporter and cheerleader, such love is felt for you. The Heavens know that you have been through much and will continue until your part is completed on the Stage of this Earth Bound Play House.

The Heavens see your tears and feel your joys with you. Your cheeks are kissed with Angel Essence to remind you that you are loved so very dearly, far more than any Earth bound word could impart.

You are encouraged to walk tall and know that you are on the path that you have chosen to walk and that the Angels walk beside you each step of the way.

When you are at your lowest of your own inner ebb the Angels are the breezes that brush your hair to remind you to look up and remember The Creator who hears ever word you utter.

When you are at the peak of your summit in joy the Angels share in your glory. You are sent butterflies to remind you that you are in the flux of change in each moment of your existence.

When you are in prayer the Angelic Presence expands your energy fields so that you can then obtain and spread more of The Creator's love and share it with the Universe.

When you are in pain the Angelic Realm waits for your invitation to assist.

When you are in need the Angelic Presence awaits your request to commune with your inner spirit, sharing with it that you are never alone.

When you are at peace, the Angelic Realm smiles and knows that you have heard its prayer for you today.

You are loved so very very much and The Angels Walk Beside You every step of the way.

I Am Archangel Michael, The Creator's Messenger of Love, Joy, Wisdom, Light, Peace & Grace.

Chapter 12
Suggested Reading List

I'll share with you some of the books that have had the most direct impact upon my awakening. Remember that what we find in books are triggers of re-membrance that assist us in finding and fitting together the puzzle of who we really are.

Since you have all your most perfect answers within your knowingness already all you need are the triggers to stimulate that information to come forth.

All Kryon Books,
By Lee Carol

All Three Conversations With God Books,
 By Neale Donald Walsh

"Anatomy Of The Spirit",
By Dr. Caroline Myss

"The Tenth Insight" (actually all of James Redfield's books have been wonderful)

By James Redfield

"Inspired by Angels"
By Sinda Jordan

"Many Were Called Few Were Chosen"
& Also " Perfect Power in Consciousness"
By Dr. Heather Anne Harder

"Ask Your Angels"
By Alma Daniel, Timothy Wyllie, and Andrew Ramer

"Commune With The Angels"
By Jane M. Howard

All materials by Dr. Deepak Chopra

All material by Dr. Wayne W. Dyer

All material by Mary Summer Rain

There are many many others, the above authors have written particularly poignant material that I have been guided to read you might share the same nudging if desired.

About the Author
Carolyn Ann O'Riley

The Author has had a passion for writing and drawing since she was a small child. This has proven to be her spiritual mission during this lifetime.

Her articles & poetry have been published in magazines, books, journals, within greeting cards and many other types of media.

The Author's artwork and designs have been exhibited in shows as well as used by such prestigious establishments as the famed Mansion on Turtle Creek.

The Spiritual Road that the Author now finds herself traveling is one of being a channel through which Archangel Michael is bringing forth messages from The Creator for those that resonate to their beautiful words.

Archangel Michael's messages have traveled around the world and back again again many times. They are being translated into other languages and published within other formats.

The books, writings, tapes, and art are dedicated to The Creator and The Creator's Messenger, Archangel Michael. They are for all ages, and peoples, no matter the race, creed, origin, religion, or culture. These books and messages are from the Universal Spiritual Heart and written in the Universal Spiritual Language of Love. They are appropriate for <u>All.</u>

Other Archangel Michael Titles By Carolyn Ann O'Riley

For All Ages:
"The Journey Within Book I of the Collection Archangel Michael Speaks". 2nd Edition: 1-4116-7931-8 ISBN

"When We Quiet Our Fears We Find Love" Book III of The Collection " Archangel Michael Speaks" ISBN 1-891870-09-2 the 2nd Edition will have a revised ISBN #

"Go Within Feel The Love" ISBN 1-891870-00-9 Book

"Go Within Feel The Love " ISBN1-891870-13-0 Audio Cassette Book on Tape

"The Remembrance of I AM, An Inner Journey of Self Discovery. A Channeled Course From Archangel Michael." Edition 2 ISBN 1-4116-6886-3

Meditation Tapes:
Healing & Releasing Meditation ISBN 1-891870-11-4

Meditation of Transformation ISBN 1-891870-12-2

The Creator's Lap of Golden Energy ISBN 1-891870-15-7

Remembrance of The Golden Light ISBN 1-891870-16-5

The Tree House of Inner Peace ISBN 1-891870-18-1

Through The Looking Glass ISBN 1-891870-19-X

Children's Collection Below The First Messages that Archangel Michael sent especially for Children

"Look Inside" ISBN 1-891870-01-7 Book A collection of 7 **rhyming lesson stories.** Most Appropriate for Ages 3 years to 7 years

Another Book By Carolyn Ann O'Riley:

"**The Lady of Court Square The Biography of Eva Caroline Whitaker Davis A Lady of Courage That Would Not Accept Defeat**" ISBN 1-4116-4808-0

To order most selections go to Lulu.com http://www.lulu.com/carolyn-oriley-3. You may also order from Amazon.com, Barnes & Noble or any of your favorite bookstores. To contact The Archangel's Pen directly

The Archangel's Pen
Carolyn Ann ORiley
18794 Vista Del Sol
Dallas, Texas 75287-4023 USA
972-931-0363 Fax
214-232-7199 Phone

We invite you to view Archangel Michael's monthly messages as they are posted to our web site.

http://www.carolynannoriley.com Web site
e-mail address: To write to Carolyn
channel333@sbcglobal.net

Your Angel Journal
A Very Special Place To Keep Your Own Angel Experiences

Printed in the United Kingdom
by Lightning Source UK Ltd.
117563UKS00001D/320